PERTH

THE CITY AT A GLANCE

GW01418095

QV1

This 40-storey Harry Seidler de
in 1991. It is fronted by Charles
red whorled *Conic Fugue* sculpt.
See p056

Woodside Plaza

Architects Kann Finch's 137m glass-clad
tower arrived in 2004. It's the eco-friendly
HQ of the oil and gas company Woodside.
240 St Georges Terrace

Central Park

Perth's tallest building was designed in 1992
by Forbes & Fitzhardinge. Soaring 249m
to the tip of its mast, it is a key landmark.
See p009

City Square

Mining giant BHP Billiton now has an aptly
giant home. At the base of the building, the
1910 *West Australian* newspaper house has
been reincarnated as a restaurant.
See p009

Convention and Exhibition Centre

Overlooking the Swan River, the three-level
venue, opened in 2004, attracts more than
500,000 visitors a year to its 600 events.
See p056

Council House

Jeffrey Howlett and Don Bailey's 13-storey
modernist block, built in 1963, is covered
in 22,000 LEDs and is a true beacon at night.
See p014

Swan Bells

Technically one of the world's largest musical
instruments, the rocket-like Swan Bells caused
some disquiet when it was unveiled in 2000.
See p011

INTRODUCTION
THE CHANGING FACE OF THE URBAN SCENE

This city was established on the profits of the discovery of gold in Halls Creek nearly 2,000km away in 1885, and it just keeps getting richer, thanks to the mineral wealth that surrounds it – diamonds, coal, copper and salt, as well as oil deposits, can all be found in vast quantities. While the world was reeling from the financial crisis, Perth was busy signing more supply deals. The city is awash with self-made millionaires, and not all of them mining barons. The money knocking around is being used to build hotels, restaurants, bars, galleries and sports venues, with enough in the kitty to hire first-class architects, designers, curators and chefs.

But the city's biggest draw can't be measured in dollars. Sir James Stirling, the admiral who named Perth in 1829 after his Scottish homeland, said the area he had chosen for the city was 'as beautiful as anything I had ever witnessed'. The green expanse of Kings Park offers an elevated view of the mostly flat city and the broad Swan River, which fills with yachts at the weekend and leads to the gently rolling landscape and vines of the Swan Valley, home to more than 40 wineries. Then there are the stunning beaches of pure white sand, underneath enormous blue skies and sunsets that slide languorously into the Indian Ocean. Spend an evening on Cottesloe beach with a plate of oysters and a glass of Margaret River sauvignon blanc, and you'll soon understand why so many people have an unquenchable appetite for Perth.

ESSENTIAL INFO

FACTS, FIGURES AND USEFUL ADDRESSES

TOURIST OFFICE
Western Australian Visitor Centre
55 William Street
T 9483 1111
www.bestofwa.com.au

TRANSPORT
Car hire
Hertz
39 Milligan Street
T 133 039
Public transport
Transperth
T 9428 1900
www.transperth.wa.gov.au
Trains run from 5.30am to midnight
Taxis
Swan Taxis
T 131 330
It's safe and easy to hail cabs on the street

EMERGENCY SERVICES
Emergencies
T 000
24-hour pharmacy
Beaufort Street 24-Hour Chemist
647 Beaufort Street
Mount Lawley
T 9328 7775
www.24hourchemist.com.au

CONSULATES
British Consulate
Level 26, Allendale Square
77 St Georges Terrace
T 9224 4700
ukinaustralia.fco.gov.uk
US Consulate
4th floor
16 St Georges Terrace
T 9202 1224
perth.usconsulate.gov

POSTAL SERVICES
Post office
Shops 3 & 4
3-7 Forrest Place
T 131 318
Shipping
UPS
T 131 877

BOOKS
Geographies of Australian Heritages: Loving a Sunburnt Country? edited by Roy Jones and Brian Shaw (Ashgate)
Jasper Jones by Craig Silvey (Windmill Books)
My Place by Sally Morgan (Virago Press)

WEBSITES
Art
www.pica.org.au
Design
www.perthculturalcentre.com.au
Newspaper
www.perthnow.com.au

EVENTS
International Arts Festival
www.perthfestival.com.au
Fashion Festival
www.perthfashionfestival.com.au

COST OF LIVING
Taxi from Perth Airport to city centre
AUD$30
Cappuccino
AUD$5
Packet of cigarettes
AUD$17
Daily newspaper
AUD$1.20
Bottle of champagne
AUD$120

PERTH

Area
1,075 sq km

Population
1.4 million

Currency
Australian dollar

Telephone codes
Australia: 61
Perth: 08

Time
GMT +8

AUSTRALIA

☐ Perth
Adelaide ○
Melbourne ○
○ Sydney
Auckland ○

AVERAGE TEMPERATURE / °C

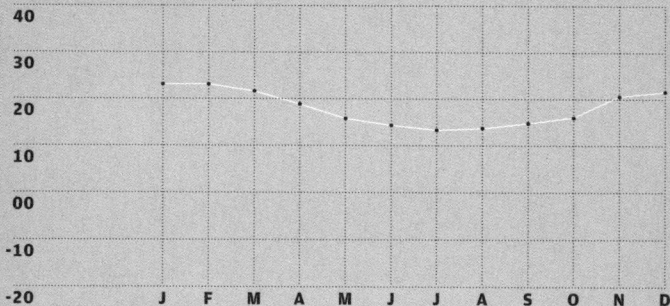

	J	F	M	A	M	J	J	A	S	O	N	D

AVERAGE RAINFALL / MM

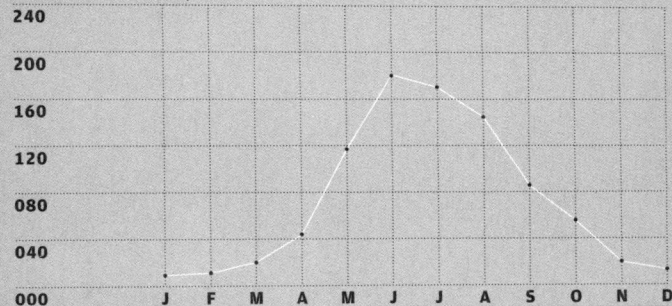

	J	F	M	A	M	J	J	A	S	O	N	D

NEIGHBOURHOODS

THE AREAS YOU NEED TO KNOW AND WHY

To help you navigate the city, we've chosen the most interesting districts (see below and the map inside the back cover) and colour-coded our featured venues, according to their location; those venues that are outside these areas are not coloured.

MOUNT LAWLEY

On Friday night, the city's workers decamp to cosmopolitan, multicultural Beaufort Street, 4km from the CBD, to bid the week farewell. There are plenty of dining options, from Italian at Cantina 663 (see p030) to Greek, Vietnamese, Indian, Spanish and French, all within a short stretch. By day, you'll struggle to recognise Mount Lawley without her LBD and heels, but boutiques such as design store Test Tube (see p080) make the trip worthwhile.

LEEDERVILLE

Here you'll find Perth's best DJs, at clubs such as Double Lucky (11/663 Newcastle Street) and The Manor (off Vincent Street, T 9272 9893). The crowd is well dressed and well behaved (naughty boys and girls go to Northbridge). Duende (see p037) and Kitsch (see p038) are perfect for a bite to eat and pre-club drinks. The historic Luna Palace Cinema (see p054) puts on outdoor screenings in the summer.

NORTHBRIDGE

It's a little rough around the edges, but this area north of the train station has got everything going for it, including the State Library, Museum, Art Gallery (see p026) and Theatre Centre (see p068). William Street's heritage buildings house fashion, arts and crafts and vintage furniture stores. You'll also find restaurants, a good selection of Vietnamese eateries, bars and clubs — this is the gay and lesbian hub.

COTTESLOE

The beach here offers a great combination of tranquil waters and lounging options, surrounded by substantial houses that come at eye-watering prices. The esplanade hosts Indiana (see p028) and Il Lido (see p040) and the wide backstreets are home to clothing store The Black Wall (30 Jarrod Street, T 6143 0365), the dine-in Lamont's Wine Store (12 Station Street, T 9385 0666) and Elba bar (29 Napoleon Street, T 9284 3482), where the champagne flows freely.

CBD

Once a soulless district that cleared out as the sun set, the city centre is now a key place to head for nightlife thanks to a clutch of new premises on and near the main drag, St Georges Terrace. There are superb modernist buildings from the 1960s and 1970s (see p014) and unique fashion finds (see p076). The 12,000-seat Perth Arena (see p088) on Wellington Street will further invigorate the area.

FREMANTLE

This industrial coastal town has been a tourist trap since the America's Cup was held here in 1987, but when day-tripper venues are as good as Little Creatures brewery (see p032) and Whisper Wine Bar (1/15 Essex Street, T 9335 7632), no one's complaining. Restaurant Harvest (1 Harvest Road, T 9336 1831) and bar Mrs Brown (see p036) in North Fremantle will keep you here longer than planned.

LANDMARKS

THE SHAPE OF THE CITY SKYLINE

Utilitarian prudence is evident in the way John Septimus Roe, the first surveyor-general of Western Australia, planned Perth in 1829. Set out on a loose grid, the deviations acknowledge the contours of the land and the meanderings of the Swan River. Yet it is Roe's setting aside of the 400-hectare Kings Park – the largest inner-city nature reserve in the world – for which locals are most grateful.

Although the city can look bland on postcards, it boasts many fine examples of Gothic, art deco and contemporary architecture. And thanks to China's appetite for Western Australia's minerals, it has the cash to continually improve its skyline. A mass of cranes is erecting skyscrapers, many of which have genuine green credentials, including recent arrivals One40william (see p060) and the 244m City Square (125 St Georges Terrace). Designed by architects Hassell and Fitzpatrick+Partners for the mining giant BHP Billiton, City Square's concrete-filled steel-tube bracing system articulates the might of the occupant and the strength of its key product.

Yet it is indicative of the nature of this city that its landmarks are quite humble – an arch (see p010), a sculpture (see p012) and a boathouse (see p015). Its tallest buildings – among them, the 247m BankWest Tower (108 St Georges Terrace) and the 249m Central Park (152-158 St Georges Terrace) – don't beg to be noticed, and much of what makes Perth great happens at street level.
For full addresses, see Resources.

Barracks Arch

First-class architects were thin on the ground in Perth in the mid-1800s, so the fledgling colony welcomed Richard Jewell when he arrived from Devon in 1852 seeking a better climate for his frail wife, Eliza. By June 1853, Jewell had been made chief of works, and the following year he created Perth Gaol – now the Western Australian Museum (see p026) – and, in 1870, the convict-built Town Hall (T 9229 2965). His red-brick Tudor-style Barracks opened in 1866 to house the red-coat guards. Inconceivably, the main building was demolished 100 years later to make way for the Mitchell Freeway. A public outcry ensured the retention of the entrance arch.
Malcolm/Elder Streets

Swan Bells

When Captain Cook completed his first round-the-world voyage in 1771, having claimed Terra Australis, the 12 bells of London's St Martin-in-the-Fields rang out; little did he imagine that they would one day peal in Perth. The Swan Bells, as they are now known, were donated to the city, along with six new models cast by London's Whitechapel Bell Foundry, to celebrate Australia's bicentennial in 1988. Some loathe the fussy design of the 82.5m copper-and-glass belfry, opened in 2000 and created by Adelaide-based architects Hames Sharley, but it has become Perth's best-known structure, and connects the city to the Swan River. Twice a week the public are invited to pull the ropes – just as well there are louvres to muffle the sound. *Barrack Square, Riverside Drive, T 6210 0444, www.swanbells.com.au*

Ascalon, St George's Cathedral

Think Anglican church garden, and you might conjure up an image of a quiet bench beneath a willow tree, or perhaps a bed of well-tended rose bushes. What you don't expect is an abstract 18m-tall sculpture of St George's billowing cloak and lance (Ascalon) thrust into the ground, sending cracks jutting across its steel base. The work of New York-based Australian sculptor Christian de Vietri and artist/curator Marcus Canning (see p052), *Ascalon* was inaugurated in early 2011 and, thanks to its progressive design and the discussion it provoked, was a local icon even before its unveiling. It has certainly put the spotlight back on Surrey-born architect Edmund Blacket's 1888 cathedral.
38 St Georges Terrace, T 9325 5766, www.perthcathedral.org

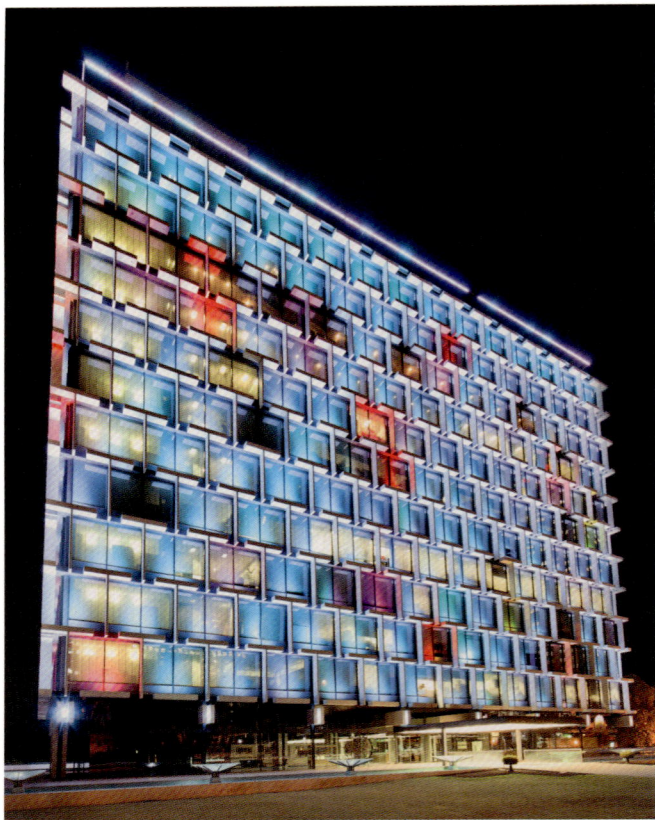

Council House

Queen Elizabeth II opened this 13-storey office block to great fanfare in 1963. It was an emblem of the city's global ambition a year after hosting the Commonwealth Games (back when they were regarded as important). Jeffrey Howlett and Don Bailey's design beat 60 other competition entries and cemented their standing as two of Australia's leading modernists. In the early 1990s, Council House was slated for demolition. It was only after a long campaign by preservationists, including James Bond set designer Ken Adam, that the building won a reprieve, and architects Peter Hunt and Daryl Jackson were commissioned to carry out an extensive restoration. It is now heritage listed, although the 22,000 LEDs turn it into a bit of a sideshow act by night. *27-29 St Georges Terrace*

Crawley Edge Boatshed

It's hard to resist the visual allure of this 80-year-old wooden boatshed that sits on the Swan River near the affluent suburb of Crawley – it's easily the most photogenic building in the city. Yet when the stilted shack was included in the sale of a nearby property in 1944, the buyers, Dr Roland and Joyce Nattrass, had to be cajoled into paying the extra £5 for it. A few owners later, it is back in the family, in the hands of the couple's son, former Perth mayor Peter Nattrass. Nearby is a bronze statue of a female bather, *Eliza*, created in 2007 by father-and-son artists Tony and Ben Jones to commemorate Crawley Baths, Perth's beloved swimming spot from 1914 to 1964.
Mounts Bay Road

HOTELS
WHERE TO STAY AND WHICH ROOMS TO BOOK

Considering the amount of spare cash that has long been swimming around Perth, it's something of a surprise that the city has only one boutique hotel, the excellent Richardson (see p022). Local entrepreneurs have all but left international chains in control and their cookie-cutter hotel rooms are a clichéd combination of chintzy bedspreads, brown décor and premixed drinks in the fridge – all in a bid to lure the business crowd. Out of these bland options, the sprawling, 367-room Hyatt Regency (99 Adelaide Terrace, T 9225 1234) is the best of the bunch.

Better news is that two promising developments are currently in progress: the government's $584m transformation of the 1874 heritage-listed Old Treasury Building (St Georges Terrace) beside St George's Cathedral (see p012) into a 46-room boutique hotel, scheduled to open in 2014; and Little Hotel, a 54-room, four-storey waterfront project by the Little Creatures brewery (see p032).

There are some excellent B&B-style establishments, but you'll have to book early to secure one of the very few rooms at the bijou Eight Nicholson (see p020) and Durack House Bed & Breakfast (7 Almondbury Road, T 9370 4305), in an Edwardian property in Mount Lawley. Such a dearth of decent beds in the city may well leave you favouring the 40-minute drive to the forested hills of Mundaring, and the delightful Core Luxury Retreat (see p018). *For full addresses and room rates, see Resources.*

Riverview

This little gem is located on one of Perth's loveliest (and steepest) streets, close to Kings Park. Built in the early 1960s to house bachelor flats, the red-brick block offers 48 self-contained studios, done out in appropriately masculine materials and tones. Those at the front have the eponymous vista but they're close to the Mitchell Freeway, so the best option is to reserve the Deluxe Suite (above) at the rear, which has midcentury-influenced furniture and a balcony with garden views. This isn't a five-star hotel, but in some ways it's the better for it. Although all studios have a kitchen (including wine glasses and corkscrew), we suggest you head downstairs to the atmospheric French restaurant Bouchard (T 9321 5013). *42 Mount Street, T 9321 8963, www.riverviewperth.com.au*

Core Luxury Retreat, Mundaring
This valley hideaway comprises a main lodge (pictured) and two stone cottages, with claw-foot baths and pot-bellied stoves, designed by architect Greg Frampton; the retreat is run by his wife, Yvonne Renshaw. Round off an afternoon by the decked pool with dinner at the nearby restaurant Loose Box (see p032). *5 Vernon Avenue, T 9295 1626, www.coreluxuryretreat.com.au*

Eight Nicholson

Interior designer Cheryl de Jong has turned her former home, an Edwardian house in Subiaco, into a wonderful haven that appears on lists of the world's top hotels. The four rooms feature dark, polished jarrahwood floors, an astute use of colour, beguiling art and design finds from around the world and underfloor heating in the bathrooms. There simply isn't a dud here, our favourite being the elegant Room 1 (opposite). The beautifully restored property is named after its address, one of the best in town; Nicholson Road stretches from Kings Park to whimsical bar The Suite (see p050) and café The Little Pantry (T 9388 8780). Before heading out, don't miss Eight Nicholson's breakfasts, ideally eaten alfresco on the terrace or in the light and airy Breakfast Room (above). *8 Nicholson Road, T 9382 1881, www.8nicholson.com.au*

The Richardson

British architect Sir Terry Farrell and local firm Cameron Chisholm Nicol designed this 74-room boutique hotel that gets everything right. Located in West Perth, The Richardson has a lobby filled with art, a spa (see p091), a wooden-decked pool and a well-equipped gym. But what really impresses is the service — the staff greet you by name and will attend to any need. Rooms are not flashy, but the basics are of a high standard: 400-thread-count cotton sheets, a choice of six types of pillow, modern bathrooms and kitchens, and a fridge stocked with provisions at corner-store prices. But don't fill up on snacks, because chef Todd Cheavins serves some of the best French fare in town at Opus (above) on the ground floor. *32 Richardson Street, T 9217 8888, www.therichardson.com.au*

Duxton Hotel

When the 306-room Duxton arrived in 1996, regular visitors to Perth breathed a sigh of relief, given the dearth of smart city-centre accommodation options. The former Australian Taxation Office, constructed in the 1970s and once the largest building in the city, was given a $32m refit by Arniston Design. The new hotel won a clutch of awards at the time, but was looking a little tired until a makeover in 2011. This is the place to stay if you want to avoid the chains without racking up too much on expenses. You'll get spacious rooms (Deluxe, above), wi-fi, a pool, a spa, good breakfasts served until late and a lovely view of the Swan River. *1 St Georges Terrace, T 9261 8000, www.duxtonhotels.com/perth*

24 HOURS

SEE THE BEST OF THE CITY IN JUST ONE DAY

Perth is the perfect 24-hour city. The business district, arts precinct and hip suburbs are tightly packed, and a trip to the seaside is a breeze. It's easy to hop between bars, restaurants and galleries, and the world's biggest inner-city area of undisturbed green space, Kings Park, is never far away. Just make sure you protect yourself from the sun with some industrial-factor cream and a panama.

Australians love a good breakfast, and there is plenty of choice in Perth – perhaps eat with a healthy conscience at Greenhouse (opposite). Once sated, soak up the art, architecture, history and literature at the Cultural Centre (see p026). The Art Gallery of Western Australia has a superbly curated collection, including work by Bill Henson and Sidney Nolan, and while you're here, take a peek at the interiors of the State Theatre Centre (see p068).

Then head to Cottesloe, to Il Lido (see p040) for lunch, and an afternoon on the beach. It's a 20-minute drive back to the city to the lively Cantina 663 (see p030) and nearby drink spot Clarences (see p047). Later, hit the clubs of Northbridge and Leederville.

If all that sounds a little too energetic, then instead head to Fremantle for a leisurely brunch at the boutique brewery Little Creatures (see p032) before sauntering aboard a ferry to Rottnest Island (see p102). In just half an hour you could be sunbathing on its white sands or scuba diving among the coral.

For full addresses, see Resources.

09.00 Greenhouse

Joost Bakker was raised on a tulip farm in Victoria and saw firsthand how restaurants pressure growers to deliver crops out of season. It inspired him to come up with a blueprint for this eco-friendly venture, which began as a pop-up in Melbourne. The green theme runs throughout. Recycled materials, such as corrugated iron, bottles and tyres, are used in the construction, and menus focus on seasonal, local produce.

The 120-seat Perth incarnation is the first permanent Greenhouse. Herbs and vegetables are grown on the roof and walls are covered with 4,000 pots of ivy. Try chef Matt Stone's wild mushroom and slow-cooked eggs on house-milled toast or salad of summer fruits, orange-blossom yoghurt and freshly rolled oats.
100 St Georges Terrace, T 9481 8333, www.greenhouseperth.com

10.00 Perth Cultural Centre

In a 300m by 250m block, you'll find the Perth Institute of Contemporary Arts (PICA; T 9228 6300); the Western Australian Museum (T 9212 3700), encompassing the 150-year-old Perth Gaol (the execution yard is now a pleasant outdoor space); the State Theatre Centre (see p068); and the Art Gallery of Western Australia (pictured, T 9492 6622). Polish-born Perth architect Kazimierz Sierakowski's Bauhaus-inspired gallery opened in 1979 and holds 17,000 works, mainly by Australian and indigenous artists. Standouts include pieces by the late Aboriginal painter Emily Kngwarreye and photographer Tracey Moffatt. PICA is housed in the 1896 Perth Central School, and stages innovative exhibitions in the former classrooms, to great effect. *James Street Mall, T 9222 8000, www.perthculturalcentre.com.au*

17.00 Indiana

Cottesloe is *the* Perth beach. As lively and beautiful as its Sydney cousin Bondi, it's a fine place for swimming, and has some superb eateries, including Il Lido (see p040). It seems impossible that the Indiana Tea House (as it was formerly known) wasn't dreamt up during the British Raj, yet this limestone blockwork building has only existed in its present form since 1996, and its handsome arches, bow window and stout corner towers are a mix of traditional and postmodern styles. Given a makeover in 2009, Indiana has become a byword for all the Gatsbyish grandeur and fun that Perth's better beaches offer. Pull up a window seat with a glass of Swan Valley bubbly, and watch the sun meet the sea.
99 Marine Parade, Cottesloe,
T 9385 5005, www.indiana.com.au

20.00 Cantina 663

Located in Beaufort Street, perhaps the most happening stretch in Perth, this canteen, which occupies part of the 1939 former Astor Cinema building by local architect William Leighton (see p057), is packed from 8am until it closes at 10pm. Its wooden tables, low stools and Thonet bentwood chairs spill out into Astor Arcade, but the attentive staff are always lightning quick with the orders.

The co-owners, chef Michael Forde and fashionista Alex Cuccovia, have created a laidback mix of distressed décor and homey Italian and Spanish tapas that draws a hip and diverse crowd. Cantina 663 is closed on Sunday evenings.
Astor Arcade, 663 Beaufort Street, T 9370 4883, www.cantina663.com

22.30 The Bird

Since it opened in 2010, The Bird has become the centre of Perth's underground scene, thanks to its programme of highly original live acts. Owners Brenton Grove and Mike O'Hanlon used old soft toys and cushions to soundproof the venue themselves, while secondhand tables and vintage leather sofas add to the grungy, super-relaxed feel. Cocktails are on the menu but this is the place to grab a local ale, perhaps a pint of Emu, from the Swan Brewery 20km outside Perth, and discover that band you've been waiting for all of your life. *181 William Street, T 6142 3513, www.williamstreetbird.com*

URBAN LIFE
CAFÉS, RESTAURANTS, BARS AND NIGHTCLUBS

The Perth scene is on the up. Top chefs are returning from stints overseas, bar and restaurant managers are striking out on their own, and big names such as Neil Perry, with his Rockpool franchise (Burswood Entertainment Complex, T 6252 1900), are arriving from out of state. Foodies flock to Blackbird (4/10 Eastbrook Terrace, T 9225 7880), for its very 'Perth' menu that draws on the city's multicultural cuisines, as well as The Loose Box (6825 Great Eastern Highway, T 9295 1787), where Alain Fabrègues' nouvelle cuisine is some of the best fare in Western Australia. Local wine is well regarded, and Perth can also boast great beer. The brewery Little Creatures (40 Mews Road, T 9430 5555) is based in a slick glass-walled building created by architect Paul Burnham, where you can enjoy its award-winning pale ale overlooking the harbour.

Northbridge's heritage buildings and (fast-disappearing) cheap rents have resulted in a rough-around-the-edges bohemian feel. For more sophistication, head west to the bars of Subiaco, such as The Suite (see p050), and Wembley, where you'll find The Stanley (see p044). St Georges Terrace is the domain of suits, heels and platinum cards. The city's best nightspot is Connections (81 James Street, T 9328 1870), the oldest gay club in Australia (Saturdays are the most mixed), but Perth is much more about live music, and at The Bird (see p031), it's beer, bands and banter until late.
For full addresses, see Resources.

Cabin Fever

This kitsch café is an unexpected find in Bon Marche Arcade, a pedestrian (in both senses of the word) lane off the bustling Murray and Hay Street malls. It opened in 2010 as an extension of the equally quirky Pigeonhole (see p076) store next door, and fast became a favourite with fashion-forward hipsters. The tiny space transports you to another world – and another decade – thanks to the woodchip floor, 1970s furniture and cuckoo clock. Owner Ruth Leigh puts her collection of antique spoons, cups and saucers to good use, serving Ristretto coffee and tea, along with breakfast, lunch and cakes until 5pm. Closed Sundays. *12 Bon Marche Arcade, 80 Barrack Street, T 9221 9837, www.cabinfever.com.au*

CNR

The grassy Northbridge piazza is a lovely space to meet, drink and chill out. A large outdoor screen shows TV programmes and films, and performances and cultural happenings take place on the stage. The CNR café completes the vibe. Designed by Perth firm Bremick, it teams vivid hues with a polished concrete floor. Five Senses coffee gives off a delicious aroma, and there's a menu of local crab, prawns, octopus and beef. There's no bar licence, but you can BYO for a corkage fee. Order out, and find a space on the grass to take in a movie.

44 Lake Street, T 9228 8861,
www.cnrnorthbridge.com

Sandwich
+
Fresh Juice
+
a piece of fruit
$16
add a coffee
+3

Mrs Brown

Hamish and Siobhan Fleming opened this Queen Victoria Street bar in 2009, the name a knowing wink to the monarch's fondness for her servant John Brown. The couple collaborated with architect Patrick Miller from local firm Finespun to create the interior. Xavier Pauchard 'Tolix' bar stools and copper-pipe lighting above the counter are teamed with Thonet bentwood chairs and vintage furniture, some from Trish's Place (T 9433 1129) next door. On cold days, sup an ale by the fire, or if the sun's out, take advantage of the garden and order a Pimm's, served in a 1940s ceramic kettle, with a plate of olives and cheese. If you're still feeling peckish, you can order in from the Flipside Burger Bar (T 9433 2188). Closed Mondays.
241 Queen Victoria Street, T 9336 1887, www.mrsbrownbar.com.au

Duende

The scent of saffron from the open kitchen at Spanish restaurant Duende instantly spirits you away from bustling Leederville. From the long list of tapas and mains, the sweetcorn and manchego fritters and calasparra rice with seafood and chorizo are signature dishes and regulars on the seasonal menu. The wine list includes full-bodied Spanish reds as well as bottles from Western Australia, and, naturally, sangria is a speciality. Owners Daniel Goodsell and Nic Trimboli (see p040) are credited with kick-starting Perth's tapas-bar boom here, and Duende remains very popular. Closed Sundays.
662 Newcastle Street, T 9228 0123, www.duende.com.au

Kitsch

Scotsman Iain Lawless is a past winner
of Australian reality show *My Restaurant
Rules*, and opened his own venture
in 2010. On the menu is a mix of Thai,
Malaysian and Singaporean dishes – the
pork dumplings are a must – and there's
a popular pad thai and Chang beer night
on Tuesdays. Lawless spent two years in
Bangkok, and his diner is inspired by the
city's street-food stalls. Tables and stools
are grouped at random in the garden,
a perfect spot for big gatherings. Inside,
clever lighting, bright colours, Oriental
tableware, bottles and bric-a-brac
help to create a bohemian atmosphere.
Closed Sundays and Mondays.
*229 Oxford Street, T 9242 1229,
www.kitschbar.com.au*

Il Lido

Nic Trimboli is one of Australia's richest men, and, as all millionaires should, he spends his time making other people happy. The co-director of Little Creatures (see p032) also owns Duende (see p037), Balthazar (see p042) and this beachfront delight. Named after the apartment block next door, the cantina serves up *cucina povera*, including excellent antipasti and handmade pasta, and features a diverse Italian wine list. The feel is casual thanks to local architect Paul Burnham's interior: communal tables, an open kitchen and bold hues, and there's a backing track of Latin beats. It's open from 8am until late, but avoid peak times in summer.
88 Marine Parade, T 9286 1111, www.illido.com.au

Moore & Moore

The limestone Moores Building was constructed in 1840, with additions made up until the 1890s. A century later, it was transformed into a contemporary art gallery with a focus on local talent, and in 2008, owner Simon Naber opened the Moore & Moore café. The historical feel has been retained, with peeling-plaster walls and exposed ceiling beams (the chandelier is a cheeky addition), and antique chairs, sofas and tables set out at random on the rough concrete floor. The café opens at 7am, and on weekdays the last order for food is taken at noon. You can't go wrong with the cooked breakfast, salads, sandwiches and pastries.
46 Henry Street, T 9335 8825,
www.mooreandmoorecafe.com

Balthazar

Located on the ground floor of the 1937 art deco Lawson Apartments building, designed by Sydney father-and-son team Hennessy, Hennessy and Associates, Balthazar opened its hefty wooden doors in 1997. As the name suggests, the restaurant is known for its impressive wine list, featuring more than 400 labels, including many from Margaret River and Clare Valley in South Australia.

Chef Scott Brannigan's Modern Australian cuisine – a style that has emerged from the collision of dishes and techniques from around the globe – ensures that Balthazar is always packed. The signature aged beef fillet is a mainstay of the meat-heavy menu. Closed Sundays.
6 The Esplanade, T 9421 1206

West End Deli

The unique 'chairdelier' created by owner Christine Peters is a quirky centrepiece but the real draw of this blue-tiled café between Northbridge and Leederville is the aroma of ground Vittoria coffee and fresh-baked bread. West End Deli is much prized by the local community, and it's not hard to see why. Drop by for a brunch of French toast, or, from Thursday to Saturday when it opens in the evenings, try the braised pork belly with pearl barley, calvados apples and crackling. The waiter station was a gift from the neighbours, and much of the furniture was won at auction or found in vintage stores.
95 Carr Street, T 9328 3605,
www.westenddeli.net.au

The Stanley

This elegant public house resembles the drawing room of a gentlemen's club. Owner Paul Fowler has proven adept at interior design, sourcing Chesterfields, chaise longues and paintings from the local vintage hubs of North Fremantle and Guildford. The space is piled high with trophies and curios – a Chairman Mao vase from Beijing, a piece of the Berlin Wall and an oar inscribed with the name Stanley that was found washed up on a Hong Kong beach. Out the back there's a courtyard lifted straight from an English country garden. The drinks are narrowed down to two key options: beer or wine – no cocktails, no fuss. Closed Mondays.

292 Cambridge Street, Wembley.
T 9387 4482, www.thestanleybar.com.au

Pata Negra

Perth's diners have long sought out the new – first it was Vietnamese cuisine, then Thai and Japanese, and now tapas. Giving Duende (see p037) a run for its money, Pata Negra became the most talked-about restaurant in town when it opened in 2009. Owner-chef David Coomer's menu is about far more than the eponymous *jamón Ibérico*, and Spanish and local bottles dominate the wine list. The authentic décor includes darkwood floors, black walls, a glass cabinet for hanging the hams and a 1940s slicer. Closed Sundays and Mondays. *26 Stirling Highway, Nedlands, T 9389 5517, www.patanegra.com.au*

Clarences

The food at Clarences is better than at many of Perth's stuffier established restaurants but it is the drinks menu that gets our vote – try the espresso martini or an alcoholic Matso's Ginger Beer out in the wooden-decked garden. Inside, there's an embossed-metal bar, leather-upholstered chairs by local furniture-maker Greg Cairns and bare brick walls. The clientele is a mix of well-dressed thirtysomethings, after-work socialisers and pre-clubbing party kids who, come midnight, hop into cabs headed for Double Lucky (T 045 073 4624) and The Manor (T 9272 9893) in Leederville or Bakery (see p052) in Northbridge. *566 Beaufort Street, T 9228 9474, www.clarences.com.au*

Helvetica

Interior designer Cristina Fego's slick space, secreted away in a two-storey warehouse, is as user-friendly as the typeface from which it takes its name. The focus is firmly on whisky, of which there are more than 80 types, although the cocktail list is pretty decent. If you're alone, take advantage of the free wi-fi.

Rear of 101 St Georges Terrace,
T 9321 4422, www.helveticabar.com

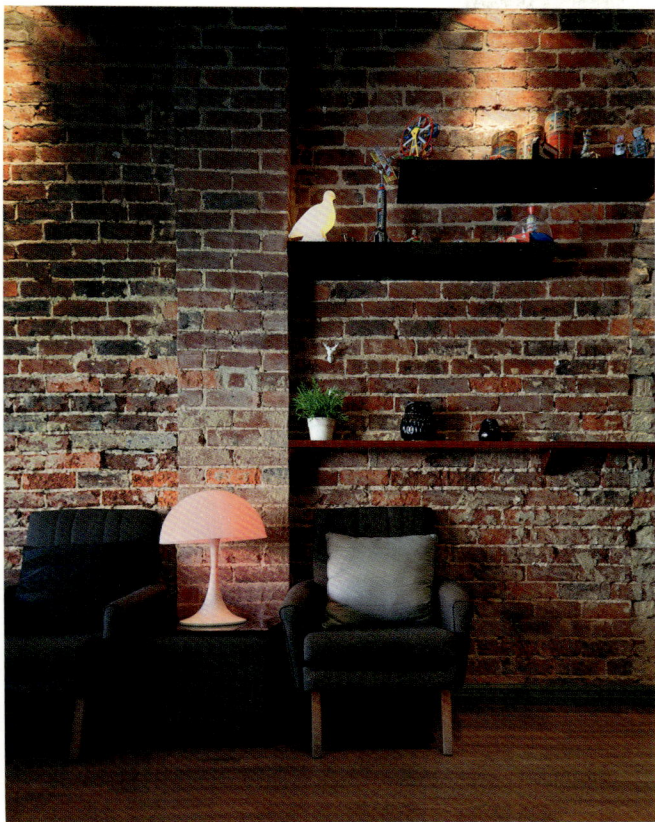

The Suite

A firm fixture of Perth's most stately suburb, Shenton Park, The Suite opens at 7am for breakfast and doesn't close until midnight. The stripped-down chic of the main room (above), with its collection of Tom Dixon 'Beat' Lights above the bar, contrasts with the more clubby side space (opposite), done out with moody green walls and vintage furnishings. It is a lively venue that functions as a café by day (breakfast is served until 3pm on Sundays), a restaurant in the evenings (the steak is recommended) and a bar at night (you can order oysters with your pint). Closed Mondays. Further along this happening street are the boutique Zekka WMN (see p086) and homewares store Fly Home (T 6380 1867).
210 Nicholson Road, T 9381 2170,
www.darkhorsedevelopments.com.au

Bakery

Artrage has been a key player in Perth's cultural landscape since 1983, and runs this cavernous venue in a former bakery that now serves up nourishment of the visual and musical kind. Director Marcus Canning, co-creator of *Ascalon* (see p012), and architect/art promoter Matt Stack refurbished the space and it reopened in 2010 as a labyrinth of black and red rooms rendered in concrete and steel.

There's a stage, a courtyard bar created from shipping containers, the Breadbox gallery and a performance studio. Beer and cider is on tap, and the house speciality is a Bloody Maria – a variation on the classic, made using tequila. Check the calendar before turning up – doors open only when there is an event.
233 James Street, T 9227 6288,
www.nowbaking.com.au

INSIDERS' GUIDE

CONOR YOUNGS AND ROMINA GIL DE MATOS

Husband and wife Conor Youngs and Romina Gil De Matos set up design store Test Tube (see p080) in 2006 before opening their fashion boutique Zekka (see p086) two years later. Its regular art installations encapsulate all that is great about the Perth scene.

The couple start the day at Elixir Coffee Specialists (45a/145 Stirling Highway, Nedlands, T 9389 9333) with a healthy breakfast and home-roasted coffee. They often have lunch at Kiri (142 Onslow Road, Shenton Park, T 9388 2727). 'It's tiny, authentic and is the best Japanese in town,' says Gil De Matos. Firm evening favourites are the buzzy Pata Negra (see p046) and Kitsch (see p038); on Friday nights, the ritual is drinks at The Stanley (see p044).

The Luna Palace Cinema (155 Oxford Street, T 9444 4056) is their favourite Perth spot, especially on summer evenings when movies are projected on to an outdoor screen. 'It's an original late-1920s cinema that shows great films,' says Youngs. They also recommend antiques hub Lauder & Howard (17 Blinco Street, T 9335 3856), and its shop-in-shop Ottoman Empire: 'We can spend hours there.'

When they have visitors, the couple drive to the Margaret River region (see p100), stopping off in Wilyabrup at wineries Pierro (Caves Road, T 9755 6220) or Knee Deep (Lot 61, Johnson Road, T 9755 6776), for a tasting and some lunch, before hitting the beach. 'Sun, sea, wine and relaxation – it's bliss,' says Youngs.

For full addresses, see Resources.

ARCHITOUR

A GUIDE TO PERTH'S ICONIC BUILDINGS

Perth architects such as Iwan Iwanoff, William G Bennett, Jeffrey Howlett and William T Leighton are known by only the keenest of students, yet they have created a beautiful urban space. In the 1960s and 1970s, the city made all the right moves. Howlett's Council House (see p014) opened in 1963 and his Concert Hall (see p063) slotted in a decade later. This was also the most fertile period for Iwanoff, the city's most famous architectural son. The 1971 Northam Library (see p096) is one of his finest works.

The influence of Adelaide architects should also be noted, from Harold Boas, who was active in Perth from 1905, to current-day practices including Hassell, responsible for City Square (see p009) and One40william (see p060), and Woods Bagot, which designed ONE30 Stirling Street (130 Stirling Street). In addition, the Vienna-born Australian Harry Seidler, who trained under Walter Gropius and Marcel Breuer, described his 1991 Bauhaus-influenced QV1 (250 St Georges Terrace) as the best building he had ever created.

The Perth Waterfront project, scheduled to begin in 2012, will flood land between the Perth Convention and Exhibition Centre (21 Mounts Bay Road, T 9338 0300) and Swan Bells (see p011), bringing the river right up to the city grid and creating a man-made island. The development includes a cultural centre, a hotel, luxury flats, shops, bars and restaurants, and a cable car to Kings Park. *For full addresses, see Resources.*

Fremantle Port Authority

The port authority building in Fremantle was designed in the International Style by local firm Hobbs, Winning & Leighton, and was inaugurated in 1964. Most visitors who take the daily guided tour do so for the views from the observation tower on top of the nine-storey building, but don't miss the mosaic work, courtyard, auditorium and dining room, with views out over the water, and the artwork by Western Australian abstract painter and sculptor Howard Taylor. Hobbs, Winning & Leighton also designed the 1962 Fremantle Passenger Terminal. Nearby is Henry Reveley's 1830 stone Round House, the state's oldest building.

1 Cliff Street, T 9430 3555

Roberts House

Bulgarian-born architect Iwan Iwanoff came to Perth as a refugee in 1950 and quickly established himself as a pioneer of modernism, responsible for about 30 buildings throughout the city. Roberts House, finished in 1967, is a signature triumph — as is his own house, not far away on Lifford Road in Floreat Park, designed the same year. Perched on a hill overlooking City Beach, Roberts House was constructed using concrete blocks. The geometric façade reinvented the blockwork concept, by turning a material chosen for its cost-effectiveness into a feature. Iwanoff extended the roof and support walls in order to shade the upper floor and wrap the house in a pocket of cool air. He also incorporated vents to catch the afternoon breeze that rolls in off the Indian Ocean. The garage is a very sympathetic recent addition.
12 Yanagin Crescent

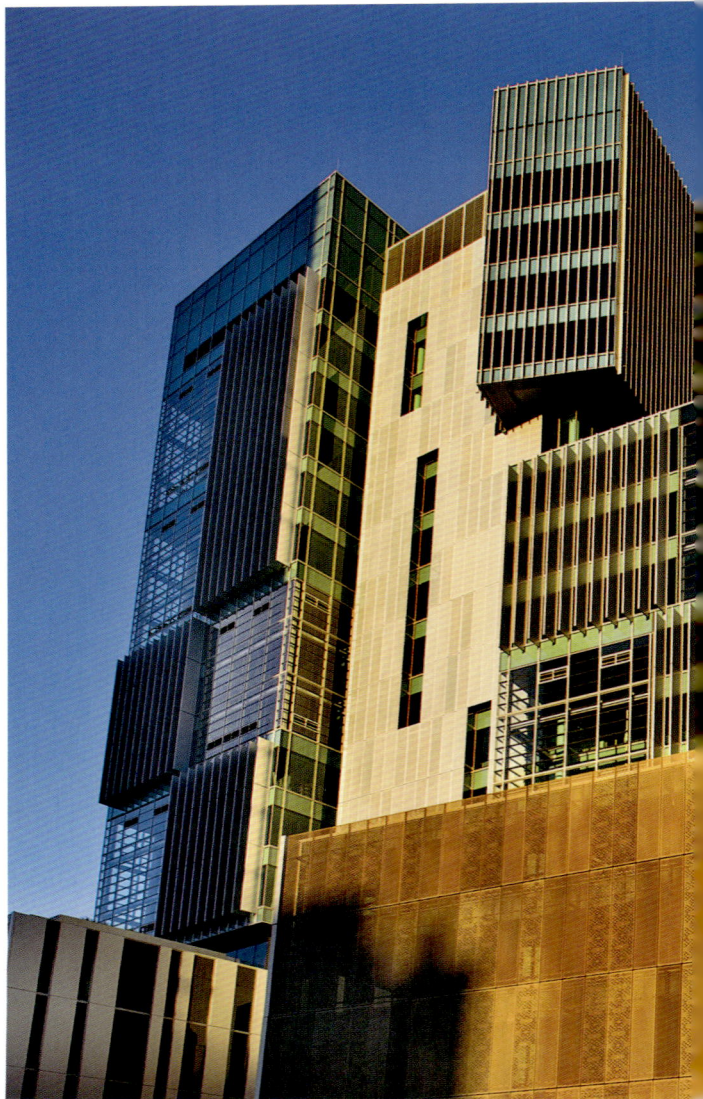

One40william

Architects Hassell's multilevel design for One40william encompasses three office towers, ranging from five to 19 floors in a stepped design, and includes 6,000 sq m of retail and entertainment space. The building, which was finished in 2010, is oriented on an east-west axis to minimise the impact of the harsh sun, one of a number of eco-friendly tricks. On the ground floor, Hassell restored three properties – the Wellington Building, the Globe Hotel and Baird's Arcade – and the 1913 façade of the Mitchell Building. The provision of bars, restaurants and rooftop gardens here has brought a neglected part of the CBD back to life. Escalators lead down to new underground Transperth platforms.
140 William Street,
www.one40william.com.au

Mount Eliza Apartments

Harold Krantz and Robert Sheldon were responsible for more flats built in Perth between 1930 and 1970 than any other practice – and changed forever its image as a city of bungalows and quarter-acre blocks. They were committed to designing high-rise apartments that workers could afford to rent, and together with star employee Iwanoff (see p058), introduced a structurally innovative contemporary European modernism that the city remains grateful for today. The circular Mount Eliza tower, which locals call the Thermos Flask, is located high on an escarpment next to Kings Park. Built in 1964, it provides a fascinating contrast to Sheldon and Krantz's neighbouring utilitarian red-brick building, Sunny Meed, completed three years previously.
71 Mount Street, West Perth

Perth Concert Hall

In 1961, as work commenced on Jeffrey Howlett and Don Bailey's Council House (see p014), the duo won a competition to create this concert hall on the other side of Supreme Court Gardens. Finished in 1973, this is brutalism as it should be: simple geometries and easily legible construction of the stripped classical style (overleaf). The sight lines from each of the 1,729 seats in the auditorium (above) are uninterrupted and acoustics are excellent. The beautiful organ is the work of Ron Sharp, who also created the instrument in Sydney Opera House. In addition to the 66 pipes on show, there are another 2,934 hidden from view. Before a performance, dine at the restaurant, refurbished by architects Palassis, to see the sun set over the river. *5 St Georges Terrace, T 9231 9900, www.perthconcerthall.com.au*

Lotterywest Federation Walkway

Designed by local firm Donaldson + Warn, the 222m elevated rusted-steel path in Kings Park, with its arched glass-and-steel bridge (above), delivers an unbeatable city vista across the Swan River. Locating the walkway is surprisingly difficult – look for the statue of Lord Forrest and then the Tuart Leaf Mosaic by London-born Perth designer Ray Leeves. The route is dotted with artwork by Nyoongar Aborigines Richard Walley and Shane Pickett. A gallery in the park sells art by the Nyoongar and other tribes from WA and the Northern Territory.
Kings Park, T 9480 3600, www.bgpa.wa.gov.au/kings-park

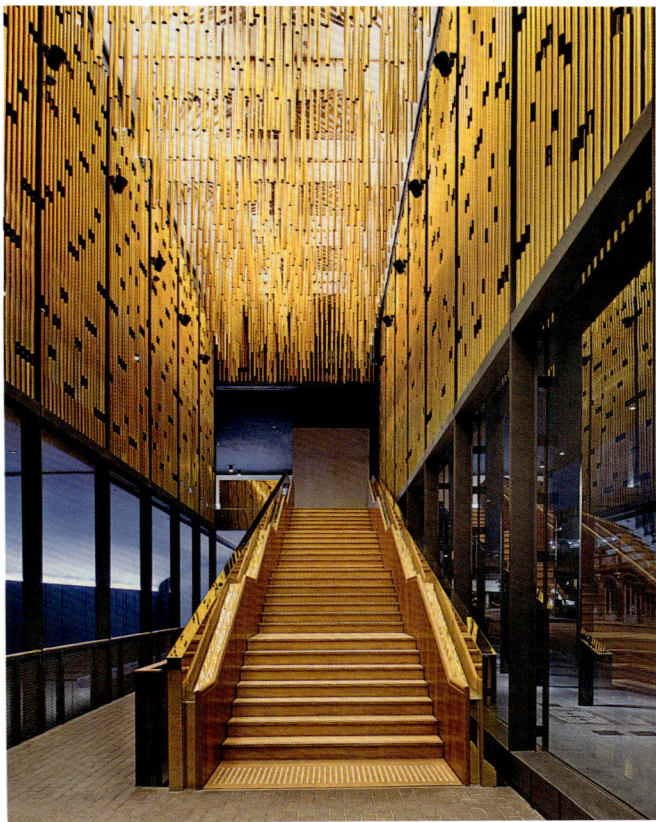

State Theatre Centre

This theatre complex, opened in 2011, was designed by Singapore architects Kerry Hill. It has a distinctive façade lined with metal fins but the foyer (above) is perhaps more striking, thanks to 1,400 gilt bronze tubes that hang from the ceiling and line the windows. Timber stairs lead up to the largest auditorium, the 575-seat Heath Ledger Theatre, a tribute to the Perth actor who died in 2008, aged just 28.

A water feature connects the theatre to the Perth Cultural Centre (see p026) and the historic buildings along William Street. *174-176 William Street, T 6212 9200, www.statetheatrecentrewa.com.au*

WA Museum – Maritime
This museum stands not far from the point where British admiral Sir Charles Fremantle stepped on to a headland 20km south of Perth in 1829 and claimed the west coast of 'New Holland' in the name of King George IV. It was designed by architects Cox Howlett + Bailey Woodland as a representation of the upturned wooden dinghy in which Fremantle's men rowed ashore, the 'stern' partly buried, the 'bow' projecting out over the water, and the overlapping panels that form the roof echoing the clinkered hull. Inside, 3,000 sq m of exhibition space documents the sea journeys made by Aborigines, as well as the illustrious trading history of the Indian Ocean port of Perth.
Victoria Quay, T 9431 8334,
www.museum.wa.gov.au/museums

SHOPPING

THE BEST RETAIL THERAPY AND WHAT TO BUY

Somehow, Perth managed to escape the mega-mall. The Sydney-based retail giant Westfield ignored the west coast in the 1960s and 1970s, leaving the creation of shopping centres to less rapacious developers. As a result, the city has managed to retain a healthy independent scene. William Street is only round the corner from the central train station, yet it's lined with more boutique stores than you can comfortably browse in an afternoon. You'll find fascinating reads by Western Australian authors at New Edition Bookshop (No 212, T 9227 0930), menswear at The Fox Hunt (No 220, T 9228 8806), art supplies at The Butcher Shop (see p074) and biodynamic skincare at Jurlique (Queens Building, No 97-101, T 9486 4753). Even in the CBD, Pigeonhole (see 076), with its three outlets, is fighting a rearguard action against the ennui-inducing Murray and Hay Street arcades. Then there's cobbled King Street, where global brands such as Gucci, Louis Vuitton and Tiffany have moved in to converted warehouse spaces dating back to the 1890s.

For epicureans, Viognier and Verdelho might not be on your shopping list before you arrive at Lancaster Wines' tin-shed cellar door (5228 West Swan Road, T 9250 6461), 30 minutes from Perth, but you'll soon be making space for a few bottles in your suitcase. The Swan Valley also boasts a chocolate factory and dozens of cafés and restaurants – and is the perfect gourmet retreat.
For full addresses, see Resources.

Venn

This design store, artists' studio and café/bar complex opened in 2011. Fashion designer Jade Rubino and freelance curator Desi Litis renovated a 1906 flour mill with local architects Matthews and interiors firm Geyer. The gallery walls are given over to Western Australians, and the shop stocks brands from around the world, including such names as Daniel Emma, Design House Stockholm and Magis.

Venn's signature Wrapping Paper Project is made in collaboration with four artists each year. The food ranges from salads to pancakes, and is served on custom-made wooden boards. Closed Sundays.
16 Queen Street, T 9481 5635,
www.venn.net

The Butcher Shop

The choice cuts at this former butcher's are the art supplies and non-traditional canvases, such as blank skate decks and ready-to-print clothing, as well as design books and magazines aimed at nurturing your creative side. Aimee Johns and Drew Turner opened this Northbridge store as an extension of Johns' now-closed Keith + Lottie Gallery in 2005. Inspired by street art and graphic design, the pair created the ad-hoc space with a nod to its original guise. The tiled back-room was turned into the retail floor, complete with slick steel counters and 1960s-style scales, and a small gallery space was added in 2011. The Staffordshire terrier Frank divides his working hours between here and the Fremantle branch (T 6420 0902).
276 William Street, T 9328 8082,
www.thebutchershop.com.au

Pigeonhole

London Court, which dates from 1937, runs between the hectic Hay Street Mall and St Georges Terrace. Lined with mock-Tudor/Elizabethan façades, it looks a little tacky, but it is home to a decent mix of retailers – notably the bijou 14 sq m Pigeonhole store. Law graduate Johann Kim started the venture in 2007, and two years later opened this third branch, which you can't miss for the orange Kronan bike outside. The interior is best described as Finnish-sauna chic – hardwood floors meet pine walls, with a painting by local artist Kyle Hughes-Odgers, aka Creepy. On sale are good-value souvenirs, stationery, accessories and the in-house jewellery range. Step in to discover an Australian designer or three. Closed Sundays.

Shop 44, London Court, 647-649 Hay Street, T 9325 1555, www.pigeonhole.com.au

Aesop

Australian brand Aesop's devotion to the pursuit of beauty doesn't stop at its botanical hair and skincare products; director Dennis Paphitis has called on some of Australia's best architectural practices to design its stores. Perth's Claremont Quarter branch opened in 2011, the work of Melbourne firm Russell & George. At centre stage is a cork-clad counter topped with sandstone hauled from the Kimberley region (see p097). The green walls complement the dark amber of the bottles, while black display cases match the labels.
Shop L1, 169 Claremont Quarter, T 9284 7638, www.aesop.com

William Topp

In 2008, Kate McKie took a punt and opened a boutique at the 'wrong' end of William Street. Conventional wisdom said no one would walk up its steep rise, but McKie has lured an intrepid army of followers by stocking designers and products, both local and international, that no one else carries. Handmade leather iPad envelopes by Madrid-based Antiatoms and origami-style bone china by Sydney's Have You Met Miss Jones are two of the standouts, along with retro finds from the 1970s and 1980s. Rewind tea and coffee, packaged locally in colourful stackable canisters, is easily transportable. Closed Mondays.

452 William Street, T 9228 8733,
www.williamtopp.com

S2

Chrissie Catling launched her S2 label in 2004. She opened this shop on the edge of Mount Lawley three years later and a second in swank Mosman Park (T 9383 1494) in 2009. Bold but minimalist, her structurally draped, layered clothes have won a loyal following not only among women; the unisex pieces are proving popular with men. As well as her own range, all tailored in Western Australia,

you'll also find select labels Lui Hon and Sosume, both from Melbourne, Sydney's Alistair Trung, jewellery by Barcelona-based French designer Sandrine de Montard and shoes by Adelaide-trained Phong Chi Lai. The pared-down boutique is Catling's work, and teams a concrete floor with white walls. Closed Sundays.
26 Angove Street, North Perth,
T 9227 1139, www.s2perth.com.au

Test Tube

This tiny product-design store is a riot of colour thanks to a vibrant wraparound timber wall that curls over to form the ceiling – the space is a collaboration between Matthews and Habitat 1. Plain box shelving showcases contemporary items from around the world, including some limited-edition pieces, and all the products have tags that tell you about the designer. You will find pots, lamps and haberdashery by Dutch designer Kiki van Eijk, 'Domsai' bonsai terrariums by Italian Matteo Cibic and ceramics by the collective Industreal, a Wallpaper* Design Award winner. Australian company Half a Teaspoon's fabulous '321' water bottle filtering system is eco-friendly and ideal to take home.

Shop 6, 595 Beaufort Street, T 9228 1118, www.testtubeobjects.com

Mr Sparrow

Collector Anna Macoboy stocks myriad products that are handmade in Australia, such as crockery by Victoria's Claystone, all-natural soaps from Queensland's Thea & Sami and her own Lulu Is A Bird range, which includes stitched cards and birdhouses made from local reclaimed wood. The colourful boxes of T2 Tea make great gifts. Postcards and a Polaroid provide information about each product and its designer. The interior of the store features more of Macoboy's fabulous finds, including vintage furniture, an old bath, an Early Kooka stove and birdcages. Mr Sparrow is closed on Sundays.
Shop 3, 223 Bagot Road, Subiaco,
T 9381 6362, www.mrsparrow.com.au

Goddard De Fiddes Art Gallery

Julian Goddard and Glenda de Fiddes have been supporting emerging Australian and international artists since 1994, and this gallery has hosted many who have gone on to great success, including Marcus Canning (see p012), illustrator Helen Smith and sculptor Jurek Wybraniec. The space is as minimal as the building it occupies – a mid-1950s modernist treat by Harold Krantz (see p062). Goddard is a co-founder of the Australian Centre for Concrete Art project (AC4CA), which supports site-specific wall art, such as a number of vast street paintings in Fremantle. Open Wednesday to Saturday. *31 Malcolm Street, West Perth, T 9324 2460, www.gdef.com.au*

Beaufort Street Merchant

Siblings Scott and Angie Taylor run this deli between Northbridge and Mount Lawley and, following popular demand, added a charming brasserie. An antique Afghan waiter station takes pride of place alongside custom-made teak tables, leather tub chairs and brass and copper lights from nearby Orno Interiors (T 9328 5556). Within the shop itself, floor-to-ceiling shelves brim with gourmet products – we're fans of the Ogilvie & Co Golden Saffron Oil, which comes in a tall, pyramid-shaped bottle, and is sprinkled with threads of saffron and gold flakes.

488–492 Beaufort Street, Highgate,
T 9328 6299, www.beaufortmerchant.com

B&M Store

If felt-loving conceptualist Joseph Beuys had ever ditched the art, he would have owned this shop, which opened in the hip west end of Fremantle in 2010. B&M is the place to go for a felt fix – covers for your iPad or iPhone, coasters, place mats and even swatches that can be used to create your own designs. The store is the idea of Jessica Williams and Jayden Weston, who create what they describe as 'way-of-life products' using 100 per cent wool from a German mill, dyed in 22 colours in an eco-friendly process. There is also a carefully curated range of stationery, books and witty items, such as the recycled-paper hunting-trophy heads (above) by US designers Cardboard Safari. *49a High Street, www.bandmstore.com.au*

Zekka

This menswear boutique and café, in a space created by architects Matthews in 2008, is the brainchild of Conor Youngs and Romina Gil De Matos (see p054). A cardboard man by sculptor Susan Flavell welcomes you in and a mural by Andrew Nicholls leads you along the corridor to the main space, where there's a light installation by Brendan van Hek. Here, you'll find Perth's hipsters sitting on Piet Hein Eek chairs and clutching cups of Five Senses coffee. Zekka and its sister store Zekka WMN (T 9388 2869) stock international labels such as MA+ by Maurizio Amadei and Rick Owens. *74-76 King Street, T 9481 1772, www.zekka.com*

SPORTS AND SPAS
WORK OUT, CHILL OUT OR JUST WATCH

Locals hit the parks to walk, run or cycle before the day heats up. On weekend mornings, Leederville and West Perth's alfresco café tables are a sea of toned bodies rewarding themselves with breakfast and a lively discussion, often about the sports they're off to watch later. Top of the list is usually Aussie Rules football. The much-loved Subiaco Oval (Subiaco Road, T 9381 2187) is home to both Perth teams, the West Coast Eagles and Fremantle Dockers, and this fast, brutal game often packs in more than 40,000 fans. The jutting angles of the 14,500-capacity Perth Arena (Wellington Street), jointly designed by Cameron Chisholm Nicol, Melbourne-based architects ARM and US firm RTKL, will bring tennis and basketball into the city centre in 2012. Golfers are in for a treat and should not miss a round at the 27-hole Joondalup Resort (Country Club Boulevard, T 9400 8811), which was designed by the world's leading course architect Robert Trent Jones Jr. The dress code is strict, so pack your argyle, plus-fours and two-tone shoes.

Of course, not all of the action is in Perth. Surfers head to Trigg Beach, just north of Scarborough, for reliable waves. If you want to join them, book a practice session with Surfing WA (360 West Coast Drive, T 9448 0004), but be aware that this is the most hazardous beach in the region. Swimmers choose Cottesloe (see p028) for its calm waters, while divers head to Rottnest Island (see p102). *For full addresses, see Resources.*

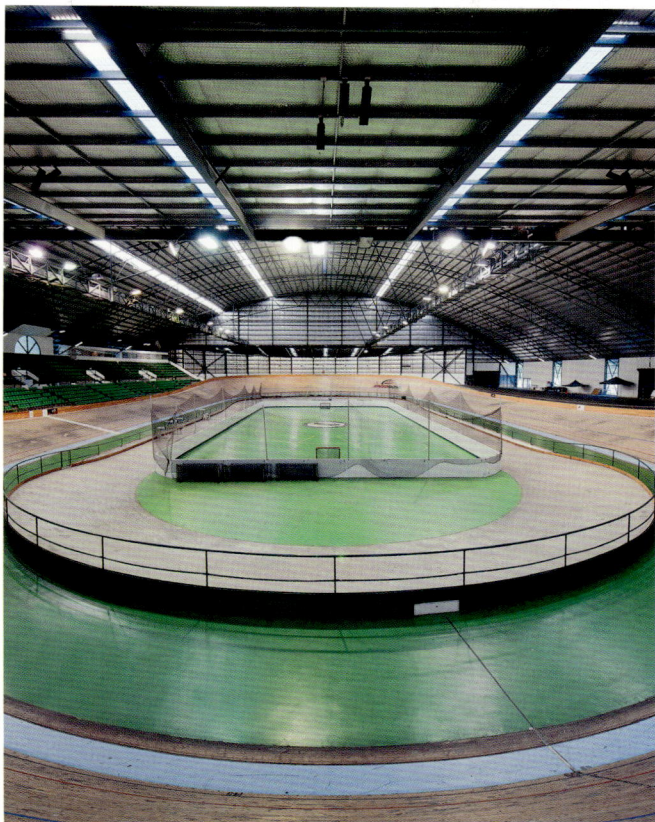

SpeedDome

This arena is the outstanding work of two masters of velodrome building. Münster-based architect Ralph Schürmann was part of the team that constructed the track used in the 1972 Munich Olympics and Australian Ron Webb designed Seoul's 1988 Olympic venue. Situated 19km from the CBD, the SpeedDome's 250m Siberian pine track has hosted many international events since opening in 1989, including the 1997 Track Cycling World Championships, but it is also a key community facility. The central area features a concrete surface that is used for roller hockey, a kickboxing gym is located under the stadium and there's also a 700m outdoor circuit.
Eddie Barron Drive, Midvale, T 9250 6701, www.venueswest.wa.gov.au

Robertson Park Tennis Centre

With the city towers as a backdrop, this club between Northbridge and Mount Lawley is a lovely setting for a knock-up on either grass, hard or synthetic courts. Racquets can be hired from the on-site pro shop, private coaching can be booked with ATP-ranked player Jason Roberts and women can sign up for Ladies Day, which combines a lesson with a doubles match. But if you're going to take on all-comers, bear in mind that this is Perth, home to 1970s Grand Slam winner Margaret Court, 1988 Olympic bronze medallist Liz Smylie and 2008 French Open doubles finalist Casey Dellacqua, so the competition could be fierce.

176 Fitzgerald Street, North Perth,
T 9328 8128, www.tenniscentral.com.au

Bicton Pool

The most fetching of Perth's superb pools is 15km south-west of the city centre, just outside Fremantle. Built on the banks of the Swan River, the outdoor venue also features a roped-off lane in the river. Bicton is home to the Melville Water Polo Club (if you're in town in December you should catch the Tom Hoad Cup) but the public can swim until 5pm during the week and from noon until 2pm at weekends, or take a therapeutic dip in the geothermal pool. Perth is not renowned for its spas, but the best place for a pamper is The Richardson hotel (see p022), where the back, face and scalp massage with hot stones is pure bliss. There are also six treatments for men, including one designed to get golfers back in the swing. *Blackwall Reach Parade, T 9339 7411, www.melvillewaterpolo.com.au*

WA Basketball Centre

The demolition of the modernist 1962 Perry Lakes Stadium in Floreat has been tempered slightly by the arrival of a sports mecca across the road at AK Reserve, 8km west of the city. The athletics track, designed by Cox Howlett & Bailey Woodland, is state-of-the-art, and the rugby centre by Sandover Pinder is aptly shaped like a hunched scrum-half. The building that scores the most points, though, is Jackson Architecture's WA Basketball Centre. Rising from the gum-tree-filled bush, the metallic, hangar-shaped building, fronted by masts and cables, opened in 2010. It can seat 2,000 spectators and has eight courts that are also used for badminton, netball and volleyball.

106 Stephenson Avenue,
T 6272 0702, www.venueswest.wa.gov.au

WACA

For many cricket fans around the world, the Western Australian Cricket Association (WACA) ground is perhaps the only reason they've even heard of Perth. The WACA has hosted Test matches since 1970, but has been a key cricket oval since its inception on a reclaimed swamp in 1893. The stadium and surrounding area is undergoing redevelopment, due to be finished in 2014, that will see residential blocks designed by local firm Christou erected around the ground – one will even sit metres from the boundary fence. These will secure WACA's financial future but come at a price for fans – the capacity will fall to 18,000. The fate of the iconic 70m floodlights is yet to be decided. *Nelson Crescent, East Perth, T 9265 7222, www.waca.com.au*

ESCAPES

WHERE TO GO IF YOU WANT TO LEAVE TOWN

One of the major disadvantages of Perth – that it's pretty much in the middle of nowhere – works in its favour once you actually arrive, as there is an almost limitless choice of unspoilt territory in the surrounding state. There's also the nagging feeling that, if you've come this far, you should really explore everything on offer. For example, in the desert, 750km north-east of Perth, you'll find Brit sculptor Antony Gormley's installation *Inside Australia*. On the dry bed of Lake Ballard, 51 eerie black steel figures look out over the landscape. The silence is as arresting as the work.

But you needn't trek so far. Wave Rock (see p098) is a popular excursion, yet few visit the nearby Hippo's Yawn and Mulka's Cave, with its 3,000-year-old Aboriginal paintings. Some 250km north of Perth in Nambung National Park are the sculptural limestone formations known as the Pinnacles. As a starting point, head to the Desert Discovery Centre (Pinnacles Drive, Cervantes, T 9652 7913), designed by Australian architects Woodhead. Much closer to the city (a mere 100km), Fitzgerald Street in Northam is home to two Iwan Iwanoff (see p058) masterpieces: the 1971 Library and 1974 Town Council Offices, which can be experienced inside and out.

When the time comes, there's only one way to leave Perth – on board the gold car of the Indian Pacific train, for the four-day trip to Sydney. There's no better way to see Australia's vast outback. *For full addresses, see Resources.*

El Questro Homestead, Kununurra

Baz Luhrmann filmed much of the epic *Australia* in the 421,000 sq km Kimberley region — one of the world's last unspoilt frontiers, with its rugged sandstone ranges, rainforest and waterfalls. Near the Northern Territory border, 3,500km north-east of Perth, you'll find El Questro Homestead, a six-suite luxury retreat with pool and tropical gardens perched atop the Chamberlain Gorge. You could easily spend a week here. Not to be missed is the boat trip up the gorge, its cliffs etched with rock art by the Wandjina tribe dating back more than 20,000 years. There's also horse-riding, and helicopter flights over the vast El Questro Wilderness Park. To get there, it's a four-hour flight to Kununurra and a 110km transfer by four-wheel drive.
75 Coolibah Drive, T 1300 863 248, www.elquestro.com.au

Wave Rock, Hyden
This is one wave you won't have trouble catching — it has been in Hyden, 340km east of Perth, for 60 million years and it's not about to break soon. The granite cliff was shaped by water erosion and stands 15m high and 110m long. Grey, red and yellow stripes run vertically along its length, changing hue a little as the sun tracks across the sky.
Wave Rock Road

Margaret River

A leisurely three-hour drive south of Perth, Margaret River has only been a wine region for 40 years, yet it's home to 200 vineyards and the local *terroir* produces award-winning cabernet sauvignon, sauvignon blanc, chardonnay, shiraz and sémillon. There are plenty of choices for tastings. In Wilyabrup, head to the biodynamic vineyard Heydon Estate (T 9755 6995), Pierro or Knee Deep (see p054). In

Margaret River itself, standouts include the oenophile's choice, Cape Mentelle (T 9757 0888), and Leeuwin Estate Winery (T 9759 0000), which has become a hub, thanks to its eaterie and art gallery, which includes works by Albert Tucker and Imants Tillers. Watershed Wines (above; T 9758 8633), by Fremantle-based architects Grounds Kent, has the best in cellar-door design. Try its zinfandel, a rare varietal in this region.

Rottnest Island

A 25-minute ferry ride from Fremantle, Rotto, as locals call it, is the classic Perth getaway. The 19 sq km vehicle-free island has no less than 63 beaches, some of which are calm and ideal for scuba diving, snorkelling and swimming, while others have reliable waves and are popular with surfers. If you're staying, opt for the boutique beachfront Hotel Rottnest (T 9292 5011) on Thomson Bay.

NOTES
SKETCHES AND MEMOS

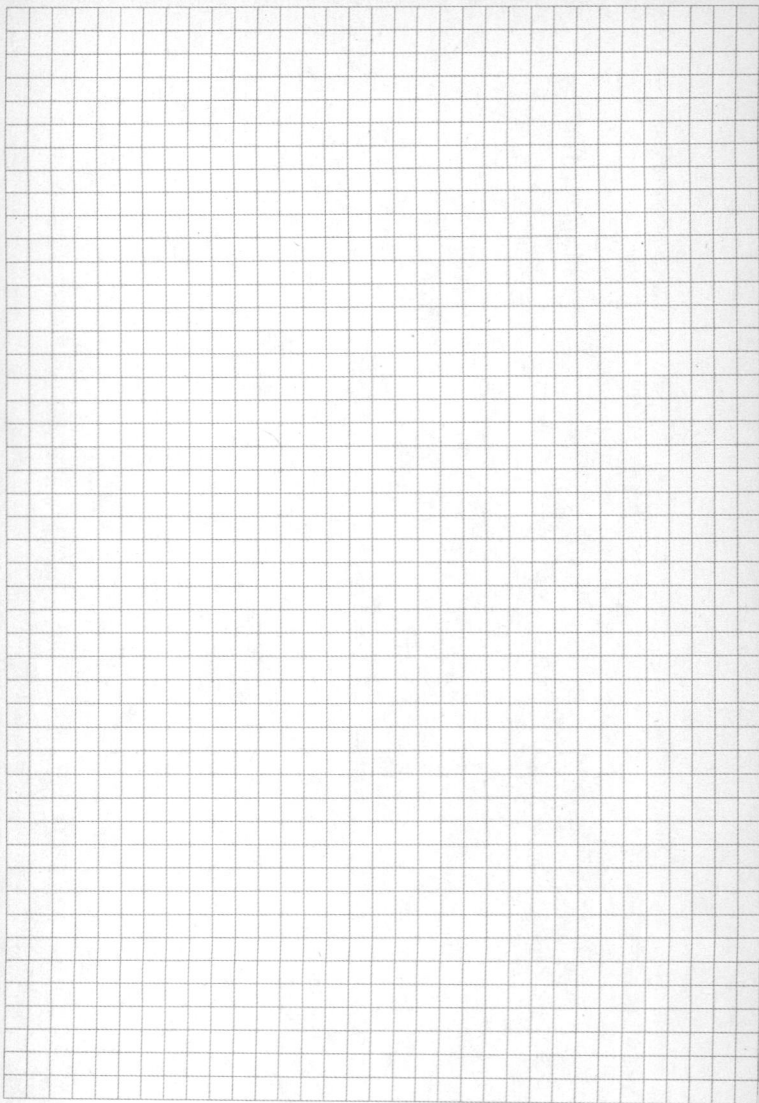

RESOURCES

CITY GUIDE DIRECTORY

A

Aesop 077
Shop L1
169 Claremont Quarter
T 9284 7638
www.aesop.com

Art Gallery of Western Australia 026
Perth Cultural Centre
James Street Mall
T 9492 6622
www.artgallery.wa.gov.au

Ascalon, St George's Cathedral 012
38 St Georges Terrace
T 9325 5766
www.perthcathedral.org

B

B&M Store 085
49a High Street
www.bandmstore.com.au

Bakery 052
233 James Street
T 9227 6288
www.nowbaking.com.au

Balthazar 042
6 The Esplanade
T 9421 1206

BankWest Tower 009
108 St Georges Terrace

Barracks Arch 010
Malcolm/Elder Streets

Beaufort Street Merchant 084
488-492 Beaufort Street
Highgate
T 9328 6299
www.beaufortmerchant.com

Bicton Pool 091
Blackwall Reach Parade
T 9339 7411
www.melvillewaterpolo.com.au

The Bird 031
181 William Street
T 6142 3513
www.williamstreetbird.com

Blackbird 032
4/10 Eastbrook Terrace
T 9225 7880
www.blackbirdrestaurant.com.au

Bouchard 017
42 Mount Street
T 9321 5013
www.bouchard.com.au

The Butcher Shop 074
276 William Street
T 9328 8082
14b Point Street
T 6420 0902
www.thebutchershop.com.au

C

Cabin Fever 033
12 Bon Marche Arcade
80 Barrack Street
T 9221 9837
www.cabinfever.com.au

Cantina 663 030
Astor Arcade
663 Beaufort Street
T 9370 4883
www.cantina663.com

Cape Mentelle 100
331 Wallcliffe Road
Margaret River
T 9757 0888
www.capementelle.com.au

Central Park 009
152-158 St Georges Terrace

City Square 009
125 St Georges Terrace
www.citysquare.com.au
Clarences 047
566 Beaufort Street
T 9228 9474
www.clarences.com.au
CNR 034
44 Lake Street
T 9228 8861
www.cnrnorthbridge.com
Connections 032
81 James Street
T 9328 1870
www.connectionsnightclub.com
Council House 014
27-29 St Georges Terrace
Crawley Edge Boatshed 015
Mounts Bay Road

D
Desert Discovery Centre 096
Pinnacles Drive
Cervantes
T 9652 7913
www.australiascoralcoast.com
Double Lucky 047
11/663 Newcastle Street
T 045 073 4624
www.doublelucky.com.au
Duende 037
662 Newcastle Street
T 9228 0123
www.duende.com.au

E
Elixir Coffee Specialists 054
45a/145 Stirling Highway
Nedlands
T 9389 9333
www.elixircoffeespecialists.com

F
Flipside Burger Bar 036
239 Queen Victoria Street
T 9433 2188
www.flipsideburgerbar.com.au
Fly Home 051
208 Nicholson Road
Shenton Park
T 6380 1867
www.flyhome.com.au
The Fox Hunt 072
220 William Street
T 9228 8806
www.thefoxhunt.com
Fremantle Port Authority 057
1 Cliff Street
T 9430 3555
www.fremantleports.com.au

G
Goddard De Fiddes Art Gallery 083
31 Malcolm Street
West Perth
T 9324 2460
www.gdef.com.au
Greenhouse 025
100 St Georges Terrace
T 9481 8333
www.greenhouseperth.com

H
Helvetica 048
Rear of 101 St Georges Terrace
T 9321 4422
www.helveticabar.com
Heydon Estate 100
325 Harmans Road South
Wilyabrup
T 9755 6995
www.heydonestate.com.au
Hippo's Yawn 096
Wave Rock Road
Hyden
T 9041 1668
www.wheatbelttourism.com

I
Indiana 028
99 Marine Parade
T 9385 5005
www.indiana.com.au

J
Joondalup Resort 088
Country Club Boulevard
T 9400 8811
www.joondalupresort.com.au
Jurlique 072
Queens Building
97-101 William Street
T 9486 4753
www.jurlique.com

K
Kiri 054
142 Onslow Road
Shenton Park
T 9388 2727
www.kirijapanese.com
Kitsch 038
229 Oxford Street
T 9242 1229
www.kitschbar.com.au
Knee Deep Winery 054
Lot 61
Johnson Road
Wilyabrup
T 9755 6776
www.kneedeepwines.com.au

L
Lancaster Wines 072
5228 West Swan Road
T 9250 6461
www.lancasterwines.com.au
Lauder & Howard 054
17 Blinco Street
T 9335 3856
www.lauderandhoward.com.au
Leeuwin Estate Winery 100
Stevens Road
Margaret River
T 9759 0000
www.leeuwinestate.com.au
Il Lido 040
88 Marine Parade
T 9286 1111
www.illido.com.au

Little Creatures 032
40 Mews Road
T 9430 5555
www.littlecreatures.com.au

The Little Pantry 020
206 Nicholson Road
Shenton Park
T 9388 8780

The Loose Box 032
6825 Great Eastern Highway
Mundaring
T 9295 1787
www.loosebox.com.au

Lotterywest Federation Walkway 066
Kings Park
T 9480 3600
www.bgpa.wa.gov.au/kings-park

Luna Palace Cinema 054
155 Oxford Street
T 9444 4056
www.lunapalace.com.au

M
The Manor 047
Off Vincent Street
T 9272 9893

Moore & Moore 041
46 Henry Street
T 9335 8825
www.mooreandmoorecafe.com

Mount Eliza Apartments 062
71 Mount Street
West Perth

Mr Sparrow 082
Shop 3
223 Bagot Road
Subiaco
T 9381 6362
www.mrsparrow.com.au

Mrs Brown 036
241 Queen Victoria Street
T 9336 1887
www.mrsbrownbar.com.au

Mulka's Cave 096
Lovering Road
Hyden
T 9041 1668
www.wheatbelttourism.com

N
New Edition Bookshop 072
212 William Street
T 9227 0930
www.newedition.com.au

Northam Region Library 096
298 Fitzgerald Street
T 9621 1600
www.northam.wa.gov.au

Northam Town Council Offices 096
395 Fitzgerald Street
T 9622 6100
www.northam.wa.gov.au

O
ONE30 Stirling Street 056
130 Stirling Street

One40william 060
140 William Street
www.one40william.com.au

Opus 022
The Richardson
32 Richardson Street
T 9217 8880
www.opusrestaurant.com.au

Orno Interiors 084
Shop 4
485 Beaufort Street
T 9328 5556
www.ornointeriors.com.au

Ottoman Empire 054
17 Blinco Street
Fremantle
T 9335 3856
www.ottomanempire.com.au

P

Pata Negra 046
26 Stirling Highway
Nedlands
T 9389 5517
www.patanegra.com.au

Perth Arena 088
Wellington Street
www.venueswest.wa.gov.au

Perth Concert Hall 063
5 St Georges Terrace
T 9231 9900
www.perthconcerthall.com.au

**Perth Convention and
Exhibition Centre** 056
21 Mounts Bay Road
T 9338 0300
www.pcec.com.au

Perth Cultural Centre 026
James Street Mall
T 9222 8000
www.perthculturalcentre.com.au

**Perth Institute of
Contemporary Arts** 026
Perth Cultural Centre
James Street Mall
T 9228 6300
www.pica.org.au

Pierro 054
Caves Road
Wilyabrup
T 9755 6220
www.pierro.com.au

Pigeonhole 076
44 London Court
647-649 Hay Street
T 9325 1555
16 Bon Marche Arcade
80 Barrack Street
T 9221 9837
7a Shafto Lane
401 Murray Street
T 9321 8112
www.pigeonhole.com.au

Q

QV1 056
250 St Georges Terrace
T 9321 5288
www.qv1perth.com

R

Roberts House 058
12 Yanagin Crescent
City Beach

Robertson Park Tennis Centre 090
176 Fitzgerald Street
North Perth
T 9328 8128
www.tenniscentral.com.au

Rockpool 032
Burswood Entertainment Complex
T 6252 1900
www.burswood.com.au

S

S2 079
26 Angove Street
North Perth
T 9227 1139
1a Glyde Street
Mosman Park
T 9383 1494
www.s2perth.com.au

SpeedDome 089
Eddie Barron Drive
Midvale
T 9250 6701
www.venueswest.wa.gov.au

The Stanley 044
292 Cambridge Street
Wembley
T 9387 4482
www.thestanleybar.com.au

State Theatre Centre 068
174-176 William Street
T 6212 9200
www.statetheatrecentrewa.com.au

Subiaco Oval 088
Subiaco Road
T 9381 2187

The Suite 050
210 Nicholson Road
Shenton Park
T 9381 2170
www.darkhorsedevelopments.com.au

Surfing WA 088
360 West Coast Drive
T 9448 0004
www.surfingaustralia.com/wa

Swan Bells 011
Barrack Square
Riverside Drive
T 6210 0444
www.swanbells.com.au

T

Test Tube 080
Shop 6
595 Beaufort Street
T 9228 1118
www.testtubeobjects.com

Town Hall 010
Barrack/Hay Streets
T 9229 2965

Trish's Place 036
243 Queen Victoria Street
T 9433 1129

V

Venn 073
16 Queen Street
T 9481 5635
www.venn.net

W

WA Basketball Centre 092
106 Stephenson Avenue
T 6272 0702
www.venueswest.wa.gov.au

WACA 094
Nelson Crescent
East Perth
T 9265 7222
www.waca.com.au

WA Museum – Maritime 070
Victoria Quay
T 9431 8334
www.museum.wa.gov.au/museums

Watershed Wines 100
Bussell Highway/Darch Road
Margaret River
T 9758 8633
www.watershedwines.com.au

Wave Rock 098
Wave Rock Road
Hyden
www.wheatbelttourism.com

West End Deli 043
  95 Carr Street
  T 9328 3605
  www.westenddeli.net.au
Western Australian Museum 026
  Perth Cultural Centre
  James Street Mall
  T 9212 3700
  www.museum.wa.gov.au
William Topp 078
  452 William Street
  T 9228 8733
  www.williamtopp.com

Z
Zekka 086
  74-76 King Street
  T 9481 1772
  www.zekka.com
Zekka WMN 086
  214a Nicholson Road
  T 9388 2869
  www.zekka.com

HOTELS

ADDRESSES AND ROOM RATES

Core Luxury Retreat 018
Room rates:
double, AUD$2,000
5 Vernon Avenue
Mundaring
T 9295 1626
www.coreluxuryretreat.com.au

Durack House Bed & Breakfast 016
Room rates:
double, AUD$190
7 Almondbury Road
T 9370 4305
www.durackhouse.com.au

Duxton Hotel 023
Room rates:
double, from AUD$210; ·
Deluxe Room, from AUD$230
1 St Georges Terrace
T 9261 8000
www.duxtonhotels.com/perth

Eight Nicholson 020
Room rates:
double, AUD$270;
Room 1, from AUD$270
8 Nicholson Road
T 9382 1881
www.8nicholson.com.au

El Questro Homestead 097
Room rates:
double, from AUD$1,265
75 Coolibah Drive
Kununurra
T 1300 863 248
www.elquestro.com.au

Hyatt Regency 016
Room rates:
double, AUD$205
99 Adelaide Terrace
T 9225 1234
perth.regency.hyatt.com

The Richardson 022
Room rates:
double, AUD$490
32 Richardson Street
T 9217 8888
www.therichardson.com.au

Riverview 017
Room rates:
double, from AUD$130;
Deluxe Suite, AUD$160
42 Mount Street
T 9321 8963
www.riverviewperth.com.au

Hotel Rottnest 103
Room rates:
double, from AUD$290
1 Bedford Avenue
Rottnest Island
T 9292 5011
www.hotelrottnest.com.au

WALLPAPER* CITY GUIDES

Executive Editor
Rachael Moloney

Editor
Jeremy Case
Authors
Gordon Kanki Knight
Mayu Kanki Knight

Art Director
Loran Stosskopf

Art Editor
Eriko Shimazaki
Designer
Lara Collins
Map Illustrator
Russell Bell

Photography Editor
Sophie Corben
Deputy Photography Editor
Anika Burgess
Photography Assistant
Nabil Butt

Senior Sub-Editor
Nick Mee
Sub-Editor
Melanie Parr

Editorial Assistant
Emma Harrison
Intern
Sofia Zetterstedt

Wallpaper* Group Editor-in-Chief
Tony Chambers
Publishing Director
Gord Ray
Managing Editor
Jessica Diamond

Wallpaper* ® is a registered trademark of IPC Media Limited

First published 2011
© 2011 IPC Media Limited

ISBN 978 07148 6263 7

PHAIDON

Phaidon Press Limited
Regent's Wharf
All Saints Street
London N1 9PA

Phaidon Press Inc
180 Varick Street
New York, NY 10014

Phaidon® is a registered trademark of Phaidon Press Limited

www.phaidon.com

A CIP Catalogue record for this book is available from the British Library.

PHOTOGRAPHERS

**Terry Carter/DK
Limited/Corbis**
Wave Rock, pp098-099

Robert Garvey/Corbis
Rottnest Island, pp102-103

Stephen Nicholls
Perth city view,
inside front cover
Barracks Arch, p010
Swan Bells, p011
Ascalon, pp012-013
Council House, p014
Crawley Edge
Boatshed, p015
Riverview, p017
Core Luxury
Retreat, pp018-019
Eight Nicholson,
p020, p021
The Richardson, p022
Duxton Hotel, p023
Greenhouse, p025
Perth Cultural
Centre, pp026-027
Indiana, pp028-029
Cantina 663, p030
The Bird, p031
Cabin Fever, p033
CNR, pp034-035
Mrs Brown, p036
Duende, p037
Kitsch, pp038-039
Il Lido, p040

Moore & Moore, p041
Balthazar, p042
West End Deli, p043
The Stanley, pp044-045
Pata Negra, p046
Clarences, p047
Helvetica, pp048-049
The Suite, p050, p051
Bakery, pp052-053
Conor Youngs and
Romina Gil De Matos, p055
Fremantle Port
Authority, p057
Roberts House, pp058-059
One40william, pp060-061
Mount Eliza
Apartments, p062
Perth Concert Hall, p063,
pp064-065
Lotterywest Federation
Walkway, pp066-067
State Theatre Centre,
p068, p069
WA Museum – Maritime,
pp070-071
Venn, p073
The Butcher
Shop, pp074-075
Pigeonhole, p076
Aesop, p077
William Topp, p078
S2, p079
Test Tube, pp080-081
Mr Sparrow, p082
Goddard De Fiddes
Art Gallery, p083
Beaufort Street
Merchant, p084

B&M Store, p085
Zekka, pp086-087
SpeedDome, p089
Robertson Park Tennis
Centre, p090
Bicton Pool, p091
WA Basketball
Centre, pp092-093
WACA, pp094-095

PERTH

A COLOUR-CODED GUIDE TO THE HOT 'HOODS

MOUNT LAWLEY
An abundance of international eateries and bars centres on vibrant Beaufort Street

LEEDERVILLE
This hub of high-end nightlife is where the city's most glamorous come out to play

NORTHBRIDGE
From its edgy bars to its inspiring galleries, Northbridge is Perth's cultural heartland

COTTESLOE
The locals' favourite stretch of shoreline, there's more to Cottesloe than its super beach

CBD
Impressive new builds are changing the skyline of the increasingly dynamic city centre

FREMANTLE
The city's port has an intriguing history and is a bona fide dining and drinking destination

For a full description of each neighbourhood, see the Introduction.
Featured venues are colour-coded, according to the district in which they are located.